Dedicated to

Every friendship group deserves grace and kindness.

Cover designs and illustrations by Ayan Mansoori

Paperback ISBN 978-1-7392624-4-0
Hardback ISBN 978-1-7392624-5-7
eBook ISBN 978-1-7392624-3-3

British Library Cataloguing in Publication Data.
A catalogue record for this book is available from the British Library.

Hello everyone, meet Anthony and Hannah. Hannah and I are best friends and Anthony is my next door neighbour. We live next to each other.

Anthony and Hannah always come by to my house on Saturdays to play and have lunch. Mummy always makes us our favourite snacks and Anthony helps me set the table.

Hannah and I share everything. Mummy says sharing is caring and that we should give if we have more. Hannah asked if she could have my toy, but I told her my Daddy gave it to me on my birthday.

Anthony let his friends know that he loves playing with them makes him happy. He usually leaves after lunch to spend the rest of the day with his family. "Thank you, guys for having me over, have a blessed day".

Mummy noticed that Hannah was sad and asked her, "What is the matter?" asked Anaiyah's mum. Hannah responded, "I want to play with the toy".

Mummy explained that she could play with it and taught her the value of sharing and understanding the word no.

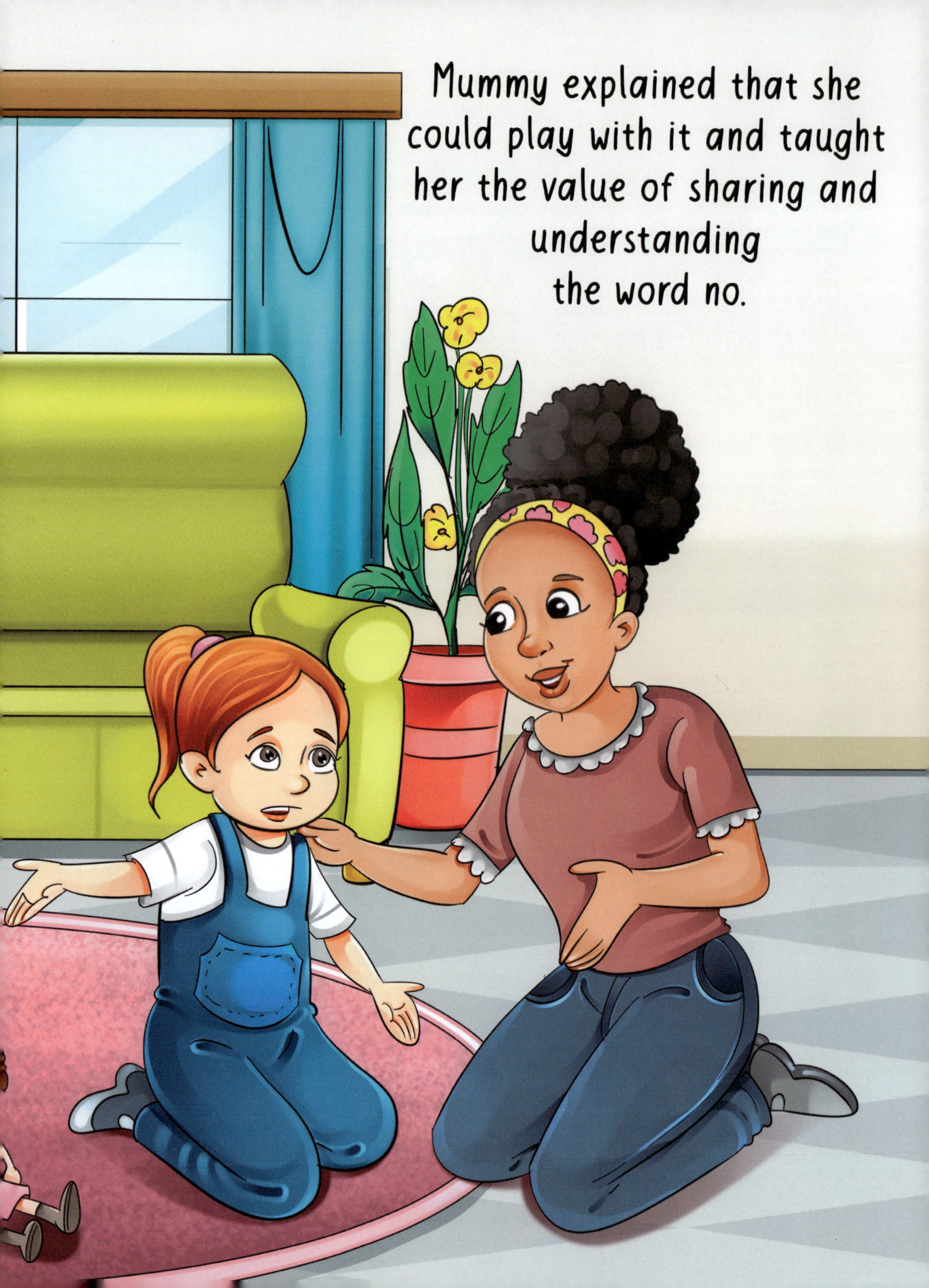

Mummy explains to Anaiyah the value of sharing and being kind to one another. Anaiyah says to Hannah, "You can play with the toy, and I am sorry for not sharing".

Mummy prayed with us
and thanked God for
our friendship and that
we continue to love one
another as God loves us.

Mummy and Daddy sat me down on the sofa and let me know that I should learn to share and be kind to others. I asked my parents if I can have a 'friends' day' where I can invite them over once a month and we pray together and play together.

Mummy said a friends day would be amazing, it is fellowship. Fellowship is where people come together and share encouraging words about Christ. A group of people learn how to live their life the way Christ did.

I decided to write an invite letter to invite my friends over to the house on Next Saturday afternoon to fellowship.

Anaiyah goes off to drop it to Anthony's letterbox and then post it to Hannah.

Anthony and Hannah both arrived at the same time and brought their favourite snacks. Mummy let us play in the garden for a while.

Mummy then told us to sit in a circle whilst I led thanksgiving. As we gathered in the living room, we all said something we were thankful and grateful for.

After the Friends Day, Daddy took Anthony and Hannah back home in the car.

A prayer from Anaiyah to her friends who are going through things and seem sad but do not know how to approach the matter.

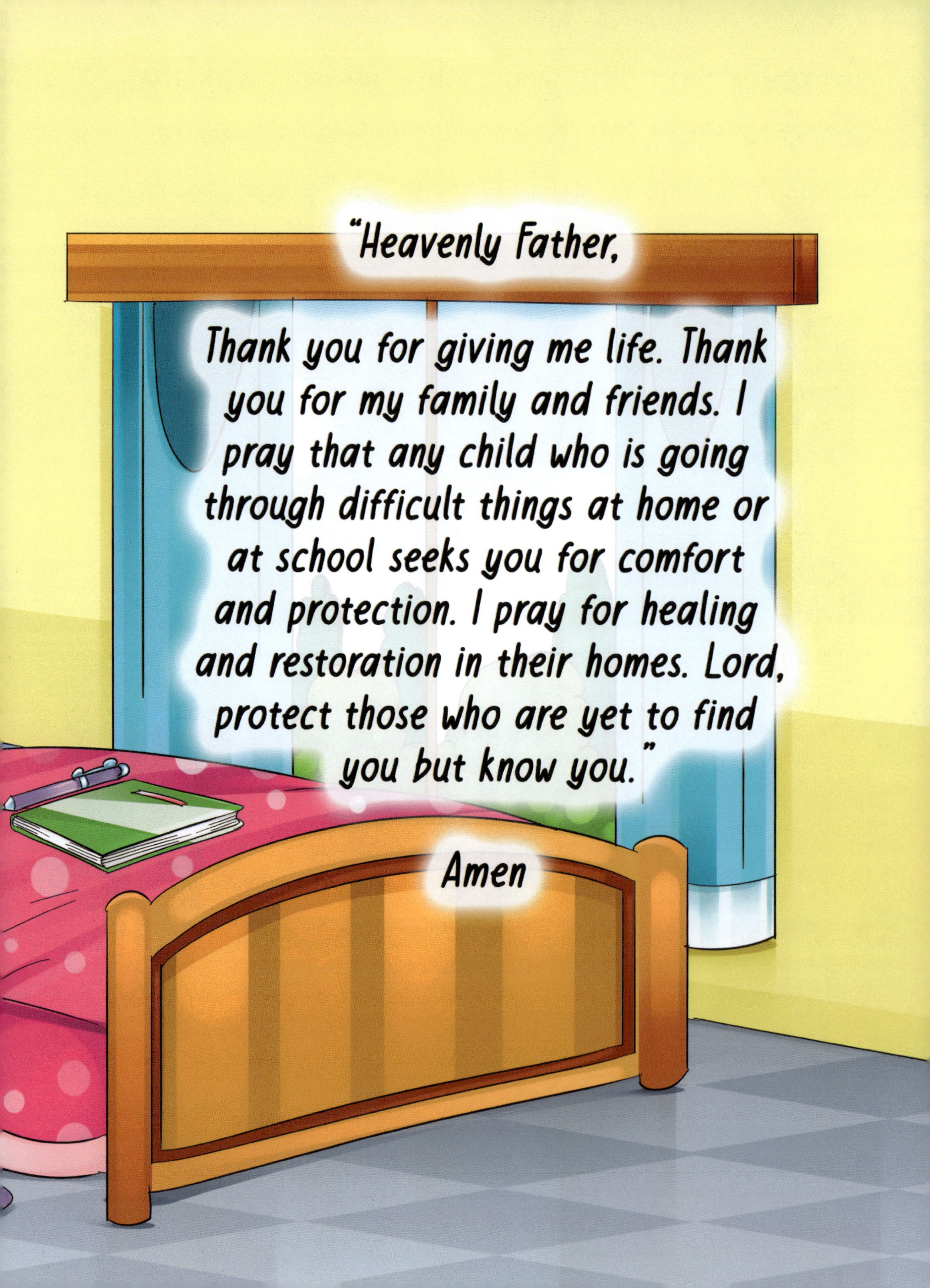

"Heavenly Father,

Thank you for giving me life. Thank you for my family and friends. I pray that any child who is going through difficult things at home or at school seeks you for comfort and protection. I pray for healing and restoration in their homes. Lord, protect those who are yet to find you but know you."

Amen

ANAIYAH & FRIENDS ACTIVITIES

Please read this scripture with me....

“Missing vowels in the words” to fill it in activity page.

‘A I E O U’

G_D

LOV_

GOSP_L

CR_AT_ON

G_N_S_S

D_C_PL_S

H_N__R

R_SP_CT

TR_ST

FR__NDS

SM_L_

GR_C

F_V__R

K_ND

N__GH_B__R

SH_R_NG

C_R_NG

H_LY

F__TH

F_RG_V_N_SS

"Kind things to say to a friend when they are in need of comfort".

"It will get better in time".

"Let's pray together".

"It is well"

"I am happy to have you as my friend".

"Everything has its season"

"I thank God for your friendship"

"God is your comfort"

ACTIVITIES-2

P	T	G	O	H	M	C	L	O	V	E	C	Z	A	A
F	O	R	G	I	V	E	N	E	S	S	E	Y	N	Z
H	T	S	X	Z	Z	C	R	C	Y	I	S	Y	T	L
U	Q	E	N	J	A	V	R	A	O	S	B	F	H	Y
K	K	W	F	T	L	E	A	R	N	I	N	G	O	Y
H	I	S	J	E	V	H	N	I	F	T	P	A	N	N
O	G	H	U	J	L	M	M	N	E	E	R	Q	Y	T
P	W	A	V	J	H	L	P	G	R	B	A	H	Z	J
E	Q	R	A	D	B	K	O	R	C	T	Y	A	H	K
F	B	I	K	U	W	R	C	W	G	U	E	N	Y	Y
T	Q	N	T	G	F	L	T	G	S	A	R	N	I	R
M	H	G	D	M	D	X	G	R	K	H	A	A	M	W
X	K	M	C	Z	Z	B	D	K	Y	J	I	H	Y	D
F	P	A	N	A	I	Y	A	H	J	N	A	P	F	W
H	N	R	L	F	F	A	I	T	H	Y	N	Q	H	G

FORGIVENESS
ANTHONY
HANNAH
FAITH

FELLOWSHIP
ANAIYAH
PRAYER
LOVE

LEARNING
SHARING
CARING
HOPE

ACTIVITIES-3

A	G	A	P	E	W	S	Y	L	S	L	X	U	F	P
H	G	M	Z	D	G	T	L	L	K	I	Q	W	A	I
F	O	E	C	M	T	L	R	L	A	M	D	Z	I	O
V	R	N	S	D	K	G	Q	S	W	L	G	M	T	B
V	Q	I	O	L	I	S	T	E	N	I	N	G	H	E
H	D	F	E	U	W	S	M	H	X	X	V	J	M	D
O	C	C	R	N	R	B	C	C	C	D	P	E	K	I
N	N	W	H	R	D	Z	Z	I	B	E	P	S	P	E
E	B	P	O	I	C	S	G	E	P	L	A	U	Z	N
S	Z	D	X	N	L	V	H	Q	E	L	J	S	L	C
T	U	Y	T	P	D	D	J	I	F	W	E	X	Q	E
Y	K	S	Z	U	D	E	L	J	T	W	B	S	Z	R
S	Z	I	M	J	Y	K	R	I	V	Z	B	O	A	K
S	G	W	G	Z	C	I	Q	P	K	O	K	D	W	S
Z	L	R	M	H	Q	V	R	J	G	E	C	R	E	F

FRIENDSHIP	**DISCIPLES**	**LISTENING**
CHILDLIKE	**OBEDIENCE**	**HONESTY**
WONDER	**AGAPE**	**HONOUR**
FAITH	**JESUS**	**AWE**

AUTHOR BIO

'Writing has always been and will always be a form of escapism. It has always left me feeling indescribable. Sometimes the feeling can be overwhelming and emotional but knowing that someone out there is going to understand or be impacted and view a different perspective about life experiences, that lets me know I am doing something meaningful. I write to show, and I write to be seen'.

Printed in Great Britain
by Amazon

58931566R00021